WESTWARD MIGRATIONS

By Doris Roettger

GOOD APPLE
A Division of Frank Schaffer Publications, Inc.

Senior Editor: Kristin Eclov
Editor: Lisa Schwimmer Marier
Cover and Interior Design: RedLane Studio
Illustration: Tracy LaRue Hohn
Photographs: Solomon D. Butcher Collection,
Nebraska State Historical Society
Cover Photography: Nebraska State Historical Society,
Solomon D. Butcher Collection

A Division of Frank Schaffer Publications, Inc.
23740 Hawthorne Blvd.
Torrance, CA 90505-5927

GA1700

ISBN 1-56417-994-X

Contents

About Westward Migrations

The lure of the western frontier began in the middle of the 1800s—stories about the beauty of the land, open spaces, ease of farming, and opportunities filtered their way east. Many people wanted to make a fresh start and saw migrating west as a way to do this. Some people migrated for economic reasons, some for religious or political reasons, all in anticipation of a better life.

In the 1800s and early 1900s, there were four separate migrations to the West. Each migration was different, yet all had similarities. The first people who emigrated west literally left the United States for the Oregon Territory—land owned at that time by Great Britain. These emigrants, and later the pioneers, trekked west for economic reasons. Land was for the taking, farming was easier, and the climate was not as harsh.

It was in February of 1846 when the first group of Mormon pioneers left Nauvoo, Illinois, en masse, to migrate west. The Mormons, or Latter Day Saints, went west for religious and political reasons, settling in Utah.

Discovery of gold and the possibility of getting rich quickly prompted the adventurous from the eastern half of the United States to head for California as quickly as they could. This third migration was called the California Gold Rush. A fourth group, children from New York, were put on the Orphan Trains west, hoping to find new families.

The westward migrations of the 1800s are important historically to the settlement of the western part of the United States. As students actively research the migrations, they will be learning information that complies with the United States history educational standards. These standards enable students to understand the United States territorial expansion between 1801 and 1861 as well as how the migrations affected relations with external powers and Native Americans.

Modeling thinking strategies and providing practice through an integrated curriculum will help students become observers and researchers. They will extend and demonstrate their understanding of the western migrations through reading, writing, speaking, listening, viewing, art, music, and simulation.

The activities in this guide are designed to engage students actively as they learn important concepts about the westward migrations. By focusing on a few key concepts, students are better able to make connections between what they read and what they experience in the activities surrounding this theme.

In the *Getting Started* activities, students are immersed in reading, watching, and doing activities that will pique their curiosity about the key concepts. During these activities, it is important for students to reflect on what they've learned and things they wonder about. Their "wonderings" will be the basis for their further research.

Students will form research groups around a particular concept related to the theme. Then, as teams, students will research questions they have wondered about, as well as work together to gather information, as they participate in the *Real-Life Laboratory*.

Through *Real-Life Laboratory* activities, students will gain a rich understanding of the westward migrations. They will have opportunities to develop a sense of life on the trails and the sea routes. Students will learn about the physical characteristics of the wagon trains, trails, and passages west, as well as how these physical characteristics affected the journeys. Students will gain an awareness of how men, women, and children adjusted to and survived the harsh environments. They will also have opportunities to see the similarities and differences in the migrations to Oregon, Utah, California, and the Midwest.

Throughout the activities, connections are emphasized across the curriculum. Students will use the information they gain through reading and viewing their writings, participating in simulation activities, and storytelling as they role-play.

The suggestions in this guide are hands-on and action-oriented. They are designed to help you meet the diverse needs and interests of your students as you integrate the social studies and language arts curricula, and embrace the multiple intelligences in your classroom.

The activities do not relate to one set of materials. Instead, the strategies and activities are designed to be used with any of the materials suggested in the bibliography and with those you may already have. The suggested interdisciplinary activities are also designed to be used across grade levels.

This theme unit can be used for any time length—from a week to a month or more, depending on the needs and interests of your students.

Suggested goals are provided near the beginning of this guide on pages 17 and 18. The webs on pages 7–9 present an overview of the areas in which activities are found. The key concepts are provided on page 10.

On most pages of *Westward Migrations,* there is some space for you to write reflective notes as well as ideas for future teaching. This guide is designed to be a rich resource from which you select the most appropriate learning experiences for your students.

Literacy Skills

The following literacy skills are addressed in the *Westward Migrations* theme guide.

WESTWARD MIGRATIONS

READING

1. Read both fiction and nonfiction books.
2. Read maps.
3. Read computer programs.
4. Read microfilm.
5. Read reader's theatre scripts.

WRITING

1 Keep a logbook for questions, answers to questions, and reflections.
2. Write letters.
3. Write and publish a Westward Travel Guide.
4. Write descriptions of life on the trail or at sea.

VIEWING

1. View videos.
2. View pictures.
3. View maps.

THINKING SKILLS

1. Analyze information.
2. Evaluate information.
3. Draw conclusions.

LISTENING, SPEAKING

1. Raise questions.
2. Listen to the ideas of others.
3. Listen to the writings of classmates.
4. Share ideas with a partner, small groups, or the whole class.
5. Tell stories.

Integrated Curriculum

The following integrated curriculum skills are addressed in the *Westward Migrations* theme guide.

WESTWARD MIGRATIONS

READING

1. Read both nonfiction and historical fiction books.
2. Read maps.
3. Read writings of class-mates.
4. Read reader's theatre scripts.
5. Read CD-ROM discs.

WRITING

1. Write questions and observations.
2. Write and publish a Westward Travel Guide
3. Write a letters.
4. Write descriptions of life on the trail.

THE ARTS

1. Sketch emigrants' lives.
2. Sing songs from the 1800s.

MATH

Calculate distances.

NUTRITION

Prepare foods of the emigrants and pioneers.

SCIENCE

Determine weather along the trail.

ORAL LANGUAGE

1. Raise questions.
2. Participate in group discussions.
3. Read writings of classmates.
4. Tell stories.
5. Participate in simulation activities.

SOCIAL STUDIES

1. Learn reasons why people moved west.
2. Describe life on the trails.
3. Describe the difficulties emigrants and pioneers faced.
4. Describe relationships with Native Americans.

Learning and Working Strategies

The following learning and working strategies are addressed in the *Westward Migrations* theme guide.

LEARNING TO USE STRATEGIES

1. Frame questions for research.
2. Develop concept maps.
3. Use vocabulary related to the westward migrations.
4. Read informational materials, maps, microfilm, and CD-ROMs.
5. View videos for information.
6. Reflect on information.
7. Draw conclusions.
8. Study map locations.

USING INFORMATION

1. Produce maps.
2. Give oral presentations.
3. Write descriptions and stories.
4. Write and publish a Westward Travel Guide.
5. Tell stories.
6. Participate in simulation activities.

WESTWARD MIGRATIONS

INDIVIDUAL OR COOPERATIVE WORKING GROUPS

1. List prior knowledge.
2. Generate questions.
3. Locate information.
4. Listen to classmates and speakers.
5. Analyze information.
6. Work in groups.

Key Concepts

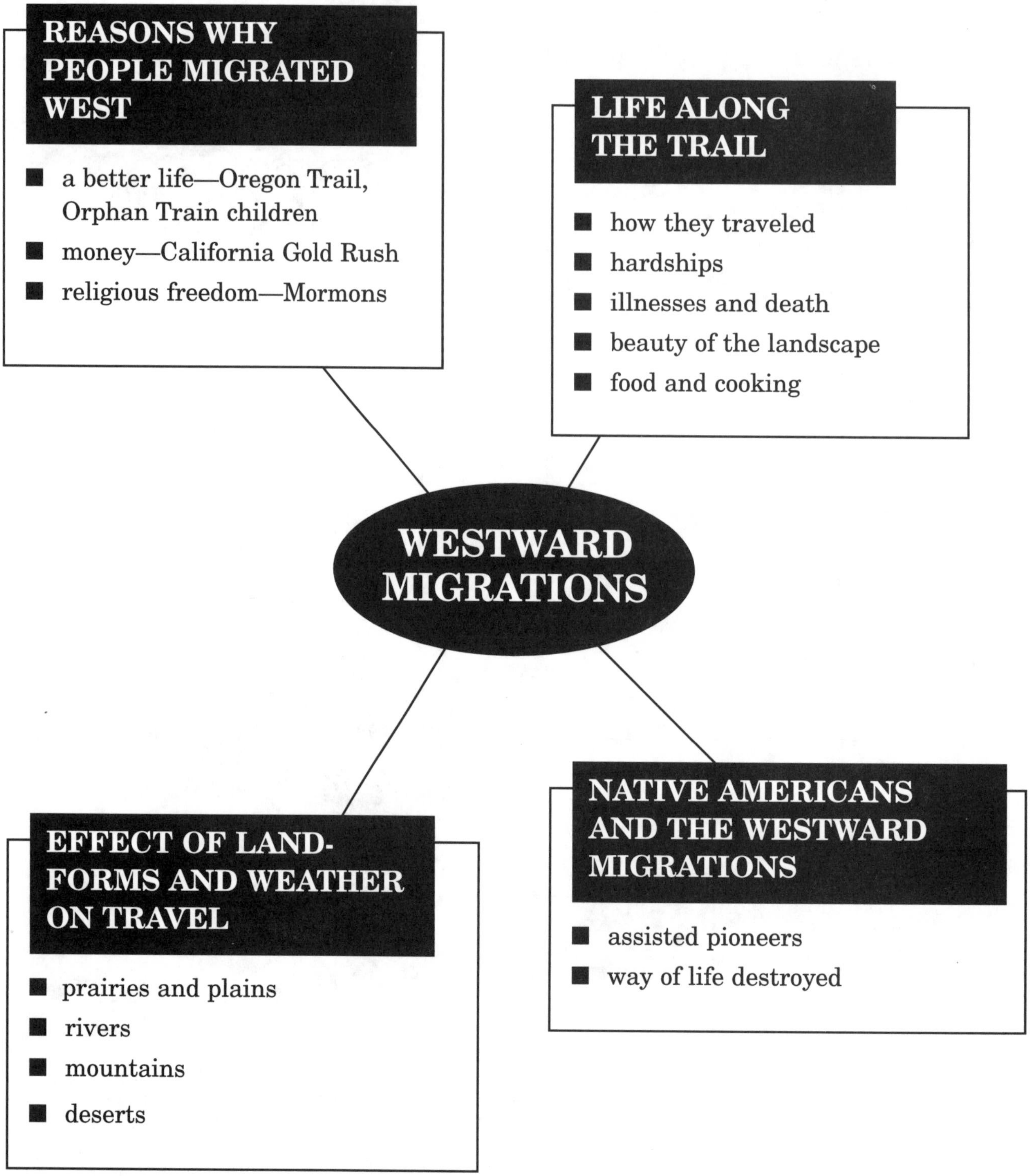

WESTWARD MIGRATIONS

REASONS WHY PEOPLE MIGRATED WEST

- a better life—Oregon Trail, Orphan Train children
- money—California Gold Rush
- religious freedom—Mormons

LIFE ALONG THE TRAIL

- how they traveled
- hardships
- illnesses and death
- beauty of the landscape
- food and cooking

EFFECT OF LAND-FORMS AND WEATHER ON TRAVEL

- prairies and plains
- rivers
- mountains
- deserts

NATIVE AMERICANS AND THE WESTWARD MIGRATIONS

- assisted pioneers
- way of life destroyed

Suggested Reading and Viewing Materials

A variety of print—both in texts and on the computer—plus viewing videos, maps, and CD-ROMs, are suggested for this theme unit. Assemble a collection of materials ahead of time. The number and types of materials you and your students use will depend on the depth and breadth of content and the length of time you plan to devote to this theme.

Nonfiction Books

Buffalo Gals: Women of the Old West by Brandon Marie Miller. Minneapolis: Lerner Publications, 1995. This book uses journals, songs, letters, and other sources to describe the experiences of women pioneers and Native American women in the American West during the 1800s.

Children of the Wild West by Russell Friedman. New York: Clarion, 1990. This resource accurately portrays life in the 19th-century American West. Life on a wagon train and the settlement of the West is told from children's points of view. Describes the effects of the wagon trains on the Native Americans as well. Includes black-and-white photos.

Daily Life in a Covered Wagon by Paul Erickson. Washington DC: The Preservation Press, 1994. This book chronicles the journey of the Larkin family from Indiana to Oregon in 1853. Each two-page chapter describes one aspect of the trip. Color pictures, quotes from family diaries, and a time line of events in the United States are included. (Easy-to-read)

If You Traveled West in a Covered Wagon by Ellen Levine. New York: Scholastic, 1992. This book uses a question-and-answer format to discuss traveling west during the 1800s. Includes information on reasons for going west, clothing, food, supplies, and daily life.

The Gold Rush by Liza Ketchum. Boston: Little, Brown, 1996. Photographs, sketches, and accounts based on primary sources help tell the stories of people who sought gold in the West as well as the affects of the migrations on the Native Americans and Spanish settlers.

The Great American Gold Rush by Rhoda Blumberg. New York: Bradbury Press, 1989. Describes life on the Overland Trail and the sea routes to California. Includes a description of the life of women. Many black-and-white illustrations help readers visualize life in California.

The Oregon Trail by Leonard Everett Fisher. New York: Holiday House, 1990. Describes vividly the emigrants' trek to Oregon. Includes descriptions of the forts and black-and-white photographs that enhance the visualization of life on the Oregon Trail.

Orphan Train Rider: One Boy's True Story by Andrea Warren. Boston: Houghton Mifflin, 1996. Chapters in this book alternate between the history of the Orphan Trains and the story of Lee Nailing, who rode the train with two of his brothers from New York City to Texas. Learn what it was like when an Orphan Train came to a small town in the Midwest.

The Pioneers by Huston Horn. New York: Time Life Books, 1974. Detailed and interesting stories of pioneers who traveled the Oregon Trail, the Mormons' trek to Utah, and the Sodbusters in Kansas and Nebraska. While the reading is difficult, all readers can learn much from the drawings, color paintings, and photographs of pioneer life.

Rocky Mountain Seasons: From Valley to Mountaintop by Diane L. Burns. New York: Macmillan, 1993. Readers are introduced to the mountain terrain through full-color photos and straight-forward information. (Picture Book)

Rough and Ready Prospectors by A. S. Gintzler. Santa Fe: John Muir Publications, 1996. The story of how "gold fever" affected the history of the West, from Sutter's Mill in 1848 to the gold rushes in other states. Maps, cartoon-like drawings, and old photos help tell the story.

Snowbound: The Tragic Story of the Donner Party by David Sievert Lavender. New York: Holiday House, 1996. A precise and horrifying account of the tragic story of the Donner Party on their trek from Illinois to California. The author gives a vivid picture of the difficulties faced by the emigrants going west. Photographs and maps are included.

The Story of Women Who Shaped the West by Mary Virginia Fox. Chicago: Childrens Press, 1991. Highlights the accomplishments of many pioneer women, including school teachers, a justice of the peace, and homesteaders.

Wagon Train: A Family Goes West in 1865 by Courtni C. Wright. New York: Holiday House, 1995. Like other African American families, Ginny's family moved from a Virginia plantation to California for a better life. Learn about the hazards of the trip, encounters with Native Americans, the never-ending chores, and their arrival in California. (Picture Book)

The Way West: Journal of a Pioneer Woman by Amelia Steward Knight. New York: Simon & Schuster, 1996. The true story of Amelia Stewart Knight, her husband, and children as they traveled from Iowa to the Oregon Territory in 1853. Written in diary style in short paragraphs. Includes brightly colored illustrations. (Picture Book)

Historical Fiction

Araminta's Paint Box by Karen Ackerman. New York: Atheneum, 1990. On the family's way to California, Araminta's uncle gives her a box of paints which is lost in an accident. This is a story of how Araminta and the paint box each journeyed west and finally met again.

Cassie's Journey: Going West in the 1860s by Brett Harvey. New York: Holiday House, 1988. Cassie describes her family's journey west. Travel with Cassie from Illinois to the soft green valley of Oregon, and experience the hardships and friendships of the trip. (Picture Book)

Dear Levi: Letters from the Overland Trail by Elvira Woodruff. New York: Knopf, 1994. A twelve-year-old boy on his way to Oregon to see his Pa's claim writes letters to his younger brother in Pennsylvania, describing his journey. The story was inspired by the diaries of people who traveled the Oregon Trail. (Includes biblical references.)

A Family Apart by Joan Lowery Nixon. New York: Bantam Books, 1987. When their mother cannot support them any longer, Francis and her siblings are sent from New York City to a mission in St. Joseph, Missouri, to live with farm families.

Train to Somewhere by Eve Bunting. New York: Clarion Books, 1996. Marianne and her four-year-old sister, Nora, are heading west with twelve other children on the Orphan Train in hopes of being placed with a caring family. Marianne fantasizes that her mother will be at one of the stops to meet her. (Picture Book)

Westering by Alice Putnam. New York: Lodestar Books, 1990. A stray dog named Scout follows eleven-year-old Jason, traveling with his family to Oregon. Jason tries hard to prove that Scout is valuable, but Scout continually gets into trouble. A heartwarming story about a boy and his dog on the dangerous trek to Oregon.

Nonfiction Books for Read-Alouds

Black Women of the Old West by William Loren Katz. New York: Atheneum, 1995. The author uses old records, newspaper clippings, pioneer reminiscences, and frontier photographs to tell the story of black women who escaped from slavery.

The Forgotten Heroes: The Story of the Buffalo Soldiers by Clinton Cox. New York: Scholastic, 1993. This book recounts the history of the 9th and 10th cavalry regiments made up of black men and formed to fight the Native Americans. The Buffalo Soldiers protected the white settlers, escorted wagon trains, built forts, and carried the mail when no one else could get through.

Pioneer Children on the Journey West by Emmy E. Werner. Boulder, CO: Westview Press, 1995. Primary sources include eyewitness accounts of approximately 120 children and young people on the California Trail between 1841 and 1865. Diaries, letters, and journals supplemented by reminiscences were written on the trail or shortly after arrival at their destination by young people in their early and middle teens.

They Saw the Elephant: Women in the California Gold Rush by Joann Levy. Hamden, Ct: Archon Books, 1990. This book tells the stories of pioneer women who traveled to California for the gold rush. Excerpts from letters, diaries, and reminiscences detail coping with adversity, courage, and a sense of freedom and happiness. These stories will captivate students' interest.

Song Books

There are a number of song and music books that contain folk songs sung on the westward migrations. Check the books you have in your classroom or check with a librarian. Look for books such as:

Folk Music in America by Terry E. Miller. New York: Garland Publishers, 1986.

Golder Encyclopedia of Folk Music by Lewis Publishing. New York: H. Leonard Publishing, 1986.

CD-ROM

The Curriculum Resource by News Bank, Inc. Find out more information about this CD-ROM by contacting <www.newsbank.com> on the Internet. Or you can call (800) 762-8182.

Oregon Trail II, Anniversary Edition. SoftKey, Multimedia Jr., 1996. CD-ROM for Macintosh and Windows.

Internet Web Sites

The following web sets provide a great deal of information and links to information about westward migration.

The Oregon Trail at <http://www.isu.edu/~trinmich/oregontrail.html>

The Overland Trail Home Page at <http://www.moore-information.com/overland>

Disc

TimeLiner 4.0 Tom Snyder Productions Inc., Watertown, MA. Grades K–12 for Macintosh or Windows. Includes program disc and back-up license, data disc of sample time lines, and teacher's manual.

Maps

Map of the Oregon Trail. National Historic Oregon Trail Interpretative Center. Flagstaff Hill, Baker City, OR 97814. Includes an information packet. (541) 523-1843.

Microfilm

Local Climatic Data (LCD). National Climatic Data Center. Request average temperatures for locations named in guide for a specific time period for the current year.

Records of the Surgeon General's Office. Records of Weather from 1819–1911 and *Meteorological Reports of the Signal Office and the Weather Bureau,* from 1860's–1902. Request temperatures for locations named in guide for a specific time in the 1840s, 1850s, and 1860s.

Microfilm is available from government depository libraries which include many state and large private university libraries, large city public libraries, and state libraries.

You can also contact the National Climatic Data Center, Customer Service Federal Building, 151 Patton Ave., Ashville, NC 28801-5001. (704) 271-4800. Ten pages of hard copy are available for a minor fee.

Reader's Theatre Scripts

Reader's Theatre, "Children's Literature Web Guide" on the Internet at <http://www.acs.ucalgary.ca/~dkbrown/readers.html>. This website gives you access to Reader's Theatre scripts, stories, and more. The Children's Literature Web Guide also contains other sites for children's literature that may interest you.

Spotlight on Reader's Theatre, "Moving West." Distributed by Phoenix Learning Resources, 2349 Chaffe Drive, St. Louis, MO 63146. (800) 822-4536. Comes in a set of 10 copies.

Videos

The Orphan Train.
A made-for-TV movie available on video.

West to Oregon: Along the Oregon Trail. ED Mellink Associates, 1993. VHS 60 min. View the life and geography of the westward migrations on the Oregon Trail between 1840 and 1870. Beautiful scenery and diary excerpts are interspersed throughout the video.

Instructional Goals

Both content and process goals are listed. Space is also provided so that you may add your own individual goals as well.

Content Instructional Goals

By the end of this theme, students should know:

1. about some of the people who migrated west.
2. where these emigrants and pioneers came from and where they eventually settled.
3. that people moved west for economic, religious, and political reasons in anticipation of a better life.
4. what life was like on the Oregon, California, and Mormon Trails.
5. the difficulties, mishaps, and hazards the emigrants and pioneers faced.
6. the effect the rivers, plains, and mountainous terrain had on the emigrants' travels.
7. some of the stories about children of the Orphan Train.
8. more about the relationships between the emigrants and the Native Americans, how the settlements of the emigrants and pioneers affected the lives of the Native Americans, and the change in the relationships between the emigrants.

Additional Goals

1. ______________________________

2. ______________________________

3. ______________________________

Process Instructional Goals

By the end of this unit, students should be able to:

1. frame questions for research.
2. develop concept maps.
3. read and view informational resources to explore and search for answers to questions.
4. collaborate with peers in research.
5. take notes.
6. maintain a log of important information.
7. write in the role of a character.
8. participate in a simulation in character.
9. tell stories in character about experiences.

Additional Goals

1. ______________________________

2. ______________________________

3. ______________________________

GETTING STARTED

Raising Curiosity

The following activities are designed to immerse students in the key concepts of *Westward Migrations*. The purpose of these activities is to arouse students' curiosity about each of the concepts. You may choose to read excerpts from books, magazines, or other resources to serve as a motivator and help children become more familiar with the theme (see the bibliography on pages 11–16). As students participate in the *"Getting Started"* activities, they will raise questions they want answered. Therefore, it is important to provide time for students to participate in most or all *"Getting Started"* activities. Open the floor to questions and comments as you and your students take part in these activities, and be sure to provide plenty of opportunities for students to choose resources independently during the activities as well as other time periods.

1. Setting Up a Resource Center

Set up a center in the room to give students a place to study and have hands-on opportunities to review materials, use resources, and log their observations about migration. You will find the following materials useful with this theme.

- Books, both nonfiction and fiction, listed in the bibliography on pages 11–16. Include travel books as well.
- Videos listed in the bibliography and a video player.
- Computer and CD-ROMs.
- Maps: current maps of the United States as well as maps showing the Oregon and California Territories prior to statehood.
- Bulletin board space filled with pictures of landmarks and life on the trails.
- Bulletin board space for a large web of the theme, key concepts, and students' questions.
- Bulletin boards or other spaces in the center to post search questions, help, and resources.

2. Introducing the Theme and Key Concepts

a. Develop a large web on a bulletin board with the key concepts students are to learn. This web is found on page 10.

b. If possible, draw and post a picture or drawing of a large prairie schooner (see page 76) in the room. Place a table in front of the drawing to display artifacts from the westward migrations.

c. Explain to students that they are beginning a new theme on the westward migrations. Discuss the key concepts they will learn more about. Use the web on page 10 as a guide.

d. Introduce the time line on page 50, beginning with the year 1803.

e. Point out to students that there were a number of reasons why so many people migrated west during the 1800s.

f. Ask students to think of reasons why people might have left their homes in the eastern states to move to Oregon, California, Utah, or the Midwest.

g. As students give reasons, write their ideas on a large sheet of paper entitled *"Reasons We Think People Migrated West in the 1800s."*

3. Beginning a Logbook

a. Ask each student to bring to class some type of notebook to use as a logbook to record information. They will also log questions they would like to research throughout the study of westward migrations.

You may also have students make their own logbooks. Provide lined paper and construction paper. Students can make covers for their logbooks and staple the lined paper inside.

b. Ask students to leave wide margins on the left side of their logbook pages and double space their writing. This way, they can go back and add questions, comments, and reflections in the margins.

c. Show students how to divide their logs into sections—observations and reflections, questions and information, and resources.

d. Discuss with students the importance of describing what they view and read in their writing. Help them understand how to clearly record information as well as their observations. Model this for students. The key is to describe, describe, describe. Detail is important.

4. Visualization and Role Play

a. Hold a class meeting. Read aloud the stories on pages 51–54 of the following groups of people who migrated west.

- Emigrants and pioneers on the Oregon Trail
- Mormon pioneers
- The forty-niners
- Orphan Train riders

b. Write the name of each migration group on a large card. Place each card in the room where there is enough space for students to talk in small groups.

Then have each student draw a slip of paper with one of the four groups listed above from a bag. Students should then go to the designated place.

c. After all students are in their groups, ask them to choose one student to be the "recorder." The recorder is responsible for writing down group information, such as questions, observations, and problems. You may want to designate a different recorder in each group for each part of the unit so all students get a chance.

d. *Visualization.* Ask students to close their eyes and imagine that they are on their way west. Read the following paragraph very slowly in your best dramatic oral reading to give students time to visualize what it was like to travel to a new home. Encourage students to use their imaginations to visualize the home they left behind.

> You left your home about a month ago and are on your way west. Let your mind think back to where you lived and why you left. Where was your home? What made you decide to leave and make a new home in the West? Think about what you left behind. Think of your house, your family, and your friends. Concentrate on how it felt to say good-bye. What did you say? To whom did you say good-bye? How did you feel? Now you begin to wonder about where you are going. Will it be any better? What will you do? Will you be happy there? Will your family be happy there?

e. *Role play.* Encourage students to think about how they visualized traveling west. Then ask them to "try on" the role of a forty-niner, a Mormon pioneer, an Orphan Train child, or someone on the Oregon Trail. Give students a few minutes to think about who they are, why they went west, what they hope to find, and how they feel.

f. Ask students to share their thoughts within their groups.

g. Have students jot down their reflections in their logbooks of the people who migrated west. Ask students to write something they may be wondering about as well.

h. Invite students to share several reflections and something they wonder about. Categorize the "wonder about" questions according to the key concepts (page 10) and list them on a large sheet of paper entitled *"Possible Search Questions."* Post it in the resource center or on a bulletin board. These search questions will be the heart of students' research as you study westward migration. See page 25 for information on search questions.

5. Viewing Photographs and Pictures

a. Have on hand photographs and pictures of travel west. See the bibliography on pages 11–16 for books as sources for pictures and photographs. Pass the pictures around for students to view.

b. Encourage students to jot down in their logbooks questions they wonder about as they look at the photographs and pictures.

c. As a class, compile the questions and add them to the sheet of possible search questions.

6. Viewing Videos

a. Show a short video or a segment of a video about the Oregon Trail to enable students to visualize the people on the trail and the conditions under which they traveled.

b. After viewing the video, ask students to jot down two or three ideas they gained from the video. Encourage them to write questions they may have or wonder about in their logbooks as well.

c. Invite students to discuss the video with the rest of their group as well as any ideas and questions that came up as they watched. Ask students to share their key points within their groups. Remind the recorder in each group to record the questions. Students should group and reword questions that overlap or are repetitious.

d. Ask the recorder from each group to then share the questions with the entire class and add them to the list of possible search questions.

7. Reading Aloud

a. Each day, read aloud to the class some aspect of life on a wagon train, a steamer to California, and an Orphan Train.

b. If possible, read aloud diary excerpts found in the book *Pioneer Children on the Journey West* by Emmy E. Werner. Boulder, CO: Westview Press, 1995.

c. Invite students to reflect on the readings in their logs. Add any questions students have to the list of possible search questions.

8. Becoming Acquainted with Resource Materials

a. Introduce a variety of books, videos, and computer programs that provide information about the various aspects of the migrations to the West. Show students that there are various research materials available on:

- the people who went west;
- life on the westward trails;
- landmarks on the trails;
- the rivers, prairies, deserts, and mountains;
- illnesses and tragedies;
- encounters with Native Americans;
- the gold rush; and
- the children on the Orphan Train.

b. Provide time for students to browse and peruse the materials and topics that interest them. Encourage students to jot down resources in their logs that they want to come back to.

9. Search Questions

a. Help students cluster all the questions that have been listed on the question board. Help them to focus the questions, making them more concise.

b. Have each student choose one question that he or she would like to research and learn more about. Students can then write their particular search question in their logbooks. Each student's question should be "researchable." For example, instead of finding information on diseases on the trek west, a more manageable question is "What is cholera and why was it so deadly?"

c. As a class, categorize and post each student's question on the theme web around the appropriate content concept.

d. The emigrants and pioneers usually studied travel guides that gave them important information about all kinds of details needed for their trips.

Explain to students that the information they gather for their search questions will be used for a Westward Travel Guide written and published by the class. See pages 46–48 for more information on writing the Westward Travel Guide.

e. Check to see that students know how to locate information. Encourage them to read the tables of contents and indexes in the books and resources to locate specific sections of interest.

f. Teach students how to take notes from the materials they have read and viewed. Ensure that they list key information that helps them answer their questions as well as the source from which it came. Students can write this information in their logbooks under their search questions.

g. Encourage students to help each other while doing research by listing resources and types of information they find along the way on cards. Ask students to write their names on the cards and post them on the resource bulletin board.

10. Recording Information

a. As students continue to find information related to their search questions as they participate in the *Real-Life Laboratory* activities, ask them to record the information in their logbooks. This will become their primary source of information for the Westward Travel Guide on pages 46–48 and simulations on pages 57–75.

b. Periodically, hold small group meetings for students to share the information they are recording.

11. Introducing Vocabulary

Introduce vocabulary as new words appear either in materials students are using or in classroom discussions. Encourage students to use the new words in their speaking and writing. Invite them to write new words on large index cards and post them around the room. A reproducible list of important words and their definitions can be found on page 55.

REAL-LIFE LABORATORY

The People Who Went West

Many people migrated to the West in the 1800s, but why? Who were these people? As students research and observe the many resources provided, they will find that everyone who traveled to the West had a very specific reason—from the emigrants traveling to Oregon, the Mormons traveling to Utah, the forty-niners to California, and the train traveling west carrying orphan children. Students will gain a better understanding of the people who moved west and the connection between them.

1. The Travelers

a. The suggested activities provide a number of opportunities for students to do research individually or in small groups. The information from the activities will provide information for their search questions.

b. Hold class information sharing sessions so students can discuss what they have learned, how they learned it, and possible resources for others.

c. Develop a class-sized web or map from the information students share. Students should add to the web following their sharing sessions. This information will be useful in the simulations on pages 57–75.

2. The Prairie Schooner

a. Ask students if they know what a prairie schooner is. Show students the picture of the prairie schooner on page 76. Explain that a prairie schooner is a covered wagon drawn by horses or oxen and was used to transport families, property, and provisions in crossing the North American prairies and plains.

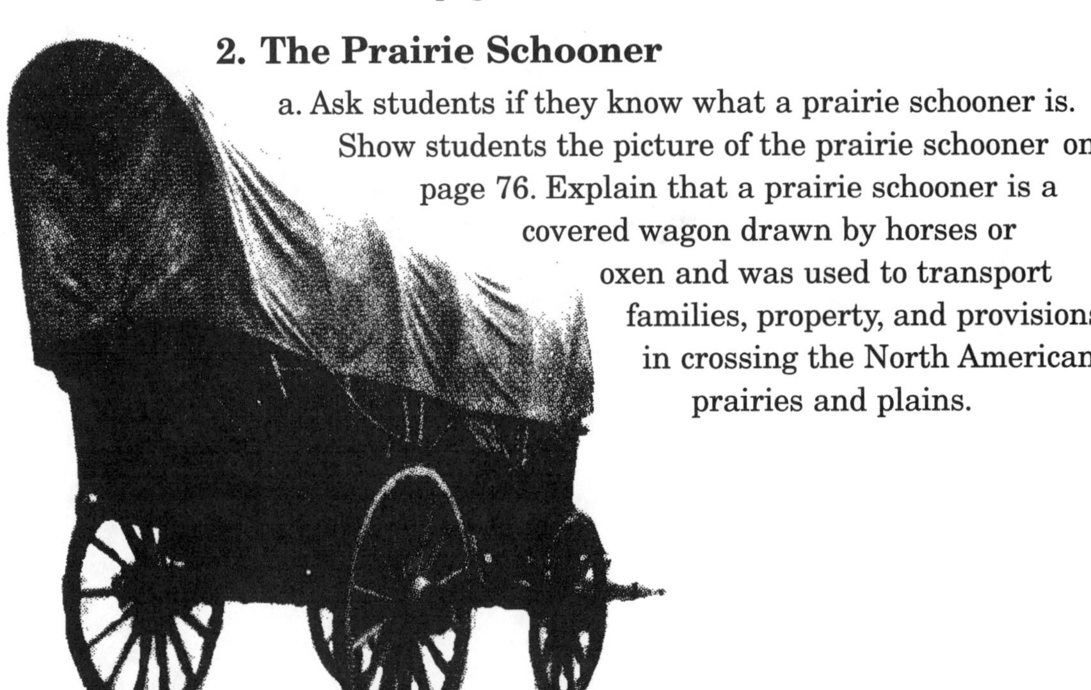

b. Have students research the dimensions of a prairie schooner. Then help them draw the schooner on a large sheet of mural paper. Tape the outline of the schooner on the floor.

c. Invite students to compare the size of a prairie schooner with a room in their homes. Hold a discussion about what their families would have to do to live in a schooner for six months. What do they think they would take along to live for six months in the schooner? Encourage students to make a list that includes foods, bedding, clothes, and everything else they think would be essential for the trip. Tell them to keep in mind the size of the schooner and how many people are in their families. Suggest students write their lists in their logbooks. Invite students to share their lists with the class.

3. The Steamer

a. Explain to the students that some emigrants and pioneers took steamships, or "steamers," to travel west by sea.

b. Ask students to find pictures of steamships from the mid-1800s.

c. Have students draw an outline on mural paper of a cabin on a steamer—ten feet long by seven feet wide. Encourage them to imagine sixteen passengers in one cabin.

d. Ask students to research and find out the sea routes to California from the east coast. What were the advantages and disadvantages of each route? What were some of the dangers? Have students research these questions and write their observations in their logbooks.

The Geography and Weather of the Overland Routes

The weather and geography of North America had a great impact on the emigrants and their travels. Provide videos, photographs, and descriptions of the land routes for students to view.

1. Geography of the Regions

a. Provide time for students to locate information about the terrain, landforms, and geography of the regions between Missouri and Iowa in the Midwest, and Utah, Oregon, and California on the west coast. This includes prairies, rivers, deserts, and mountains. Encourage students to select topics that relate to their search questions.

b. Have students map the prairies, rivers, deserts, and mountains, including the Continental Divide, on a large class map. Encourage students to complete an individual map to place in their logs.

Have students look for and include the following rivers on their maps:

- Platte River
- Sweetwater River
- Snake River
- Columbia River

c. Ask students if they know why the emigrants might have traveled along rivers. What were some of the hazards of the rivers?

d. Suggest that students learn how the emigrants crossed rivers. What gave them problems? How did they get the wagons across? How did they get the animals across? How did getting across the rivers differ according to each river?

e. Students should look for and include the following mountain ranges on their maps:

- Rocky Mountains
- Cascade Mountains
- Blue Mountains
- Sierra Nevada Mountains

f. Have students find out how the difficulties going down a mountain differed from climbing up a mountain.

g. Encourage students to look for and include desert areas on their maps. Then ask students to find out what made travel in the desert so difficult.

h. Ask students to write their reflections about the geography of the trails in their logbooks.

2. Weather on the Overland Route

a. The weather played a key role in the emigrants' and pioneers' trek west. Suggest to students that they find out what the weather was like for each of the following locations in 1844, 1852, and 1864:

Independence, Missouri	1st week of May
Fort Kearny	1st week of June
Fort Laramie	2nd week of July
Fort Boise	3rd week of August
Fort Walla Walla	4th week of September
Oregon City	2nd week of October
San Francisco	2nd week of October

b. Specific weather data can be obtained on microfilm from Government Depository Libraries, which include university libraries, large city libraries, and some state libraries. See the bibliography for specific titles of the microfilm.

Encourage students to contact the National Climatic Data Center for recent local climatic data (LCD) for the locations and dates listed above. The address and phone number for the center is on page 16.

c. Have students find descriptions of the thunderstorms, sand storms, cold nights, hot days, and snowstorms the emigrants and pioneers encountered. Ask students how they think the storms affected the wagons, cattle, and the people.

d. Form collaborative small groups of five to six students to decide how the landforms and weather for each geographical region made travel easy or more difficult for the wagon trains. Each group should present its information to the class. This information should be included in the class Westward Travel Guide.

e. Have students chart the weather of the 1800s and the weather today. How similar or different are the weather patterns for each location? Is there greater variability for one or more sites? If yes, what might be some of the reasons?

f. Ask students to write their reflections about weather on the trails in their logbooks.

3. Landmarks and Signposts

a. Ask students as they read and view materials to find and locate landmarks and signposts that the emigrants and pioneers saw, such as:

- Courthouse Rock
- Jail Rock
- Chimney Rock
- Scotts Bluff
- Independence Rock
- Devil's Gate
- Split Rock
- South Pass
- Natural Bridge
- Soda Springs, Idaho
- The Dalles

b. Based on their reading and viewing, have individual students write a short description of each landmark. Include the descriptions in the Westward Travel Guide.

c. Using today's travel books, have students find a description of these same landmarks as they are today. Ask students to add a paragraph to their descriptions for the Westward Travel Guide.

d. Determine the distance between each landmark from information in the resource books or by measuring distances on travel maps.

e. Invite students to draw, paint, or make a model of each landmark. Display student work in the classroom or on the artifacts table.

4. Plants and Animals Along the Trail

a. Have each regional terrain group find in their reading and viewing the names of plants emigrants might have seen in each region.

b. Have each group find in their reading and viewing the names of animals emigrants might have seen in each region. Some of the many animals they may have seen include:

- antelope
- buffalo
- coyotes
- grizzly bears
- owls
- prairie dogs
- snakes
- wolves

c. Encourage student groups to find pictures, draw, or paint pictures of the plants and animals.

d. Develop a bulletin board of the plant and animal pictures for each region. Or you may want to place the pictures on a large classroom map.

5. Mapping the Routes

a. Invite students to once again get into the migration groups they formed on page 31.

b. On a large classroom map, have the Oregon Trail emigrants and pioneers group mark their route from Independence, Missouri, to the Willamette Valley in Oregon.

c. In another color, ask the Mormon pioneers group to mark their trail from Nauvoo, Illinois, to Salt Lake City, Utah. Be sure students show where they followed the Oregon Trail and where the route differed.

d. In another color, have the Overland forty-niners group mark their trail west. Be sure to show where the trails to California moved away from the Oregon Trail.

e. Have the Orphan Train group mark the route of the wagon trains from New York City to the states in the Midwest where the children traveled.

f. Help students complete individual maps to place in their logbooks, showing all the routes as well.

Sea Routes to California

Some emigrants did not want to take the Oregon Trail west as others had. They were worried about the many hazards of a trip over land. They decided to get to the West by sea, though they knew this trip had its own hardships as well.

1. The Routes

a. Explain to students that a large number of easterners traveled to California by sea rather than on land.

b. Ask students to locate and mark the following routes on a large classroom world map. Help students make individual maps of the sea routes for their logs as well.

Panama Route —New York, Boston, or Charleston to the port of Chagres in Panama; along the Chagres River to the town of Gorgona; then over land to Panama City; then a ship to San Francisco.

Nicaragua Route —Eastern cities to San Juan del Norte, Nicaragua; up the San Juan River; across Lago de Nicaragua; then a ship to San Francisco.

Mexican Route —New Orleans, Galveston, Corpus Christi, New York, and Philadelphia to Tampico or Veracruz on Mexico's east coast; trek over mountains and deserts to the Pacific Coast; and then a ship to Acapulco, San Blas, or Mazatlán, Mexico; then a ship to San Diego and then San Francisco.

Cape Horn Route— New York or Boston to Rio de Janeiro, Brazil; to Cape Horn; then to Valparaiso, Chile; then to Callao, Peru; and then a ship to San Francisco.

2. Expectations and Realities

a. Have students draw a large Venn diagram.

b. Ask half of the students to find out why many easterners chose to go west by sea. What did they expect the trip by ship would be like? Have students list what they think emigrants' expectations were in the left circle.

c. Ask the other half of the students to find out what the trips on the ships were like. These students should list what the trips were like in the right circle.

d. Pair students—one from each group—to compare the expectations with the realities. When the expectations and the realities are the same, have students write them in the middle section of the diagram.

e. Hold a whole class meeting for the purpose of having partners share their findings. Were there any differences between the short and long routes by sea?

f. Ask students if they found information on advertisements for sea travel to the West. How believable and how reliable were the ads for the sea routes?

g. Ask students to jot down their thoughts in their logs about the sea routes and the people who took them to the West.

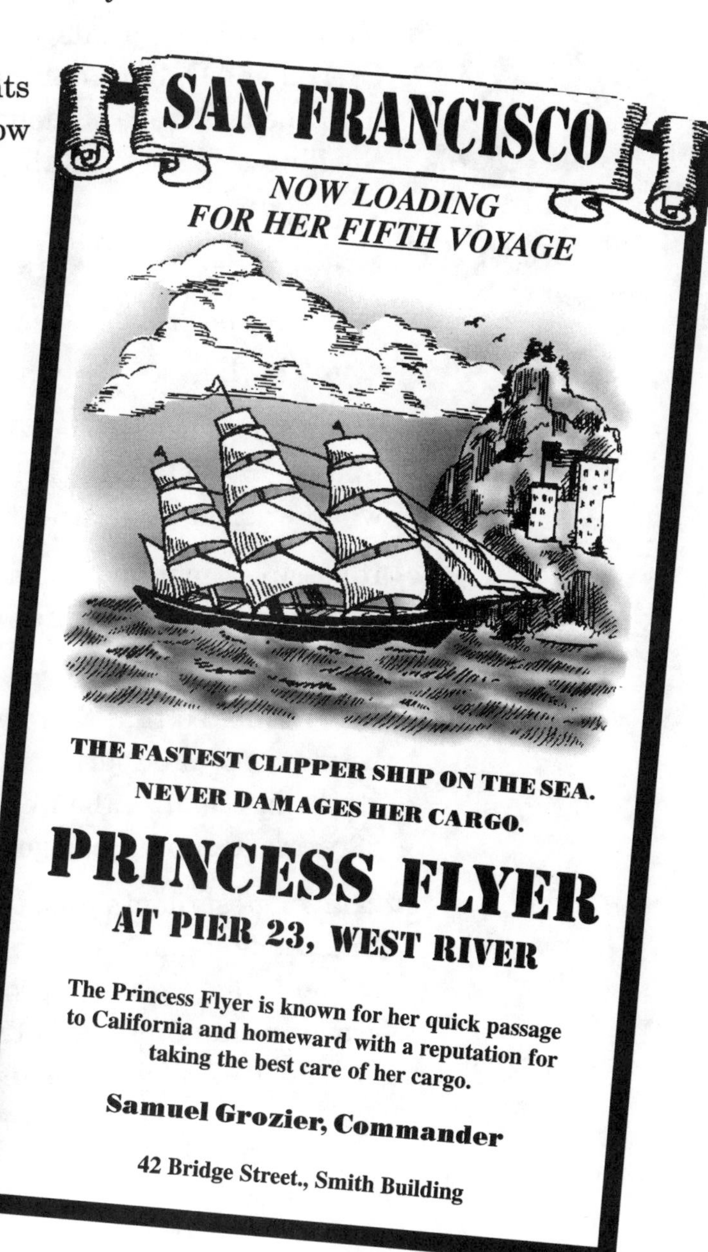

Meeting the Elephant

Hazards, Illnesses, Accidents, and Death on the Move West

"Meeting the Elephant" was a term emigrants used to describe encountering the worst conditions possible as they made their way west. Discuss with your students some of the perils that the emigrants and pioneers were up against.

1. Hazards and Illnesses Along the Trail

a. Many of the emigrants and pioneers got sick on the way to Oregon and California from illnesses and hazards such as those listed below. Have students research the illnesses. What caused the illnesses? How did they affect people?

- cholera
- dysentery
- scarlet fever
- toothaches
- measles
- snakebites
- typhoid
- malaria

b. Many times, people died from these illnesses. Ask students to find out how many of these illnesses still exist today and whether or not they are still fatal.

c. If possible, invite a pharmacist to talk with students about the effectiveness of medicines used in the 1800s and medicines used today.

d. It is estimated that there was one grave dug every 80 yards between the Missouri River and Willamette Valley. To help students visualize the number of deaths, place a marker every 80 yards around the edge of your school grounds.

e. Challenge students to determine the distance between Independence, Missouri, and the Willamette Valley in Oregon. If there was a grave approximately every 80 yards, how many graves would there be between Independence, Missouri, and Willamette Valley, Oregon?

2. Accidents Along the Trail

a. Ask students to speculate about the type of accidents that occurred along the trail as the emigrants traveled west. How do they think the accidents might have happened? As students give you their ideas, list them on a large sheet of paper and post it in the resource center.

b. As students read and view materials, encourage them to look for the type of accidents that occurred. As they find them, have them verify their speculations.

c. Ask students to think about the wagons and the types of accidents that could occur. Again, list their speculations, and then ask them to verify problems. How did the emigrants and pioneers repair the wagons when the wagons broke down?

d. Ask students what people today have to do if their car breaks down on a trip from Missouri to Oregon, California, or Utah. Who would have an easier time of it—people on the trails or people today?

3. The Donner Party

a. Ask students to research the Donner Party. How many people were in this wagon train when it started? Who were the people?

b. What happened to the group? What hardships did they encounter? Why did this happen? How many people made it to California?

c. Have students try to find the Donner Pass on a current road map of California.

4. Water

a. Explain to students that the water supply was a continual problem. Ask students for what purposes people needed water. Where did the pioneers get their water? How did the pioneers carry water? How much water do students think the pioneers could carry?

What do people use water for today? Ask students to try to find out how much water their families use each day. Students can compare the amount of water used on the trail with the amount of water used today.

b. For each of the following situations, encourage students to find out where on the trail each could have happened as well as the effects each situation had on both the cattle and the people:

- no water
- alkaline water
- polluted water

c. Encourage students to determine whether polluted water and alkaline water exists today. If so, where does it exist? What causes water to be alkaline or polluted? Can alkaline or polluted water be treated so people can drink it? How?

5. Dangers at Sea

a. Ask students to speculate about the type of accidents that may have occurred at sea on the trip west. How do they think the accidents might have happened? As students give you their ideas, list them on a large sheet of paper and post it in the resource center.

b. Ask students to think about the steamers and the types of accidents that could occur. List their speculations, and then ask them to verify problems. How did the emigrants repair the ships? Were there problems with weather? What other problems could occur on a ship sailing in the ocean? What kind of illnesses could people get while at sea?

The Wagon Trains and the Native Americans

As the wagon trains made their way west, the emigrants met people along the way whose customs and ways of living were somewhat different than their own. Help students understand the difference between myth and reality in regard to the relationships between the Native Americans and the emigrants.

1. Identifing Native American Peoples and Where They Lived

a. Have students identify the Native American people who lived between Independence, Missouri, and Oregon through whose lands the emigrants and pioneers traveled.

b. Provide each student with a copy of the Oregon Trail outline map found on page 77. Ask students to draw in the territories for each of the Native American tribes in the 1800s.

2. Recognizing Myths and Realities

a. Ask students to jot down in their logbooks their thoughts about the encounters the emigrants and pioneers might have had with the Native Americans.

b. Form small groups of three to four students so they can share their thoughts. Appoint one student in each group to record the different ideas.

c. Hold a whole class meeting so each group can present their ideas. How many students believe that the emigrants were in danger from the Native Americans? What type of danger did they think they were in? How many students believe that the emigrants were not in danger from the Native Americans? Why? Were the Native Americans in danger from the emigrants? Why?

d. Have students return to their groups. Then ask each group to select one of the Native American tribes and research how they lived in the 1800s. Find out how the Native Americans helped the emigrants through bartering or trading, guiding the wagon trains, and assisting the emigrants across rivers.

Also have students research how the relationships between the Native Americans and the emigrants and pioneers changed after the 1860s.

- Why did the relationships change?
- What effect did large groups of people moving west have on the hunting grounds, grass, buffaloes, and health among Native Americans?

e. Hold a class meeting to:

- have each group report their findings.
- talk about ways TV and old western movies depict Native Americans.
- talk about the myths and realities of the relationships between the emigrants and Native Americans.

f. Fact: During the 1840s and 1850s, approximately 250,000 emigrants and pioneers traveled the trails to Oregon and California. Only 362 pioneers were killed by Native Americans, and an estimated 425 Native Americans were killed by the pioneers. (Source: John Unrah, Jr. Historian in *They Saw the Elephant* by Joann Levy, pg. xvi.)

Foods on the Trail

The emigrants and pioneers brought foods along on their trek that wouldn't spoil—beans, flour, sugar, cornmeal, coffee, molasses, salt, as well as dried fruits, vegetables, and meats. Share with students some of the following foods the emigrants and pioneers ate on their trek west.

Cooking Foods of the Emigrants and Pioneers

a. Have students research how the pioneers were able to cook food. What did they use for fuel?

b. Make arrangements with the cafeteria personnel so you and your students can cook some of the foods the emigrants ate on the trail. Or you may decide to make these foods yourself with the help of adult volunteers as well as your students.

c. Form a committee of two to four students for each food to be made. One adult should work with each student committee.

Fried Cakes

Combine 1 1/2 cups (75 ml) flour with 1 cup (50 ml) water. Mix well with a fork. Roll out dough 1/4-inch (6 mm) thick, using plenty of flour on your hands and a breadboard. Cut into 2-inch (5-cm) squares. Render beef fat in a skillet and add squares of dough. Brown slowly on both sides. Sprinkle with salt to taste. Makes about 20 cakes. (Substitute cooking oil for the beef fat.)

Soda Bread

To make dough, mix 1 teaspoon (5 ml) baking soda with 1 cup (50 ml) warm water. Add 2 1/4 cups (63 ml) flour and 1 teaspoon (5 ml) salt. Knead well. Dough may be used at once or allowed to rise overnight in a warm place. In either case, flatten dough to a thickness of 1 inch (2.5 cm). Place on a greased cookie sheet and bake in a 400°F (205°C) oven for about 25 minutes.

Mormon Johnnycake

Combine 2 cups (500 ml) yellow cornmeal, 1/2 cup (125 ml) flour, 1 teaspoon (5 ml) baking soda, and 1 teaspoon (5 ml) salt. Stir in 2 cups (500 ml) buttermilk and 2 tablespoons (30 ml) molasses. Pour batter into a greased 9-inch (22.5 cm) pan, and bake in a 425°F (218°C) oven for about 20 minutes. Cut into 16 squares. To make a lighter cake, add 2 beaten eggs and 2 tablespoons (30 ml) melted butter to the buttermilk and bake approximately 25 minutes.

Dried Apple Pie

Soak 2 cups (500 ml) dried apples in water overnight. Drain off water and mix apples with 1/2 cup (125 ml) sugar and 1 teaspoon (5 ml) each of allspice and cinnamon. Line an 8-inch (20 cm) pie pan with a crust, add the apple mixture, dot with 3 tablespoons (45 ml) of butter, and cover with a second crust. Make a few slashes in the top of the crust for ventilation and bake in a 350°F (175°C) oven for about 1 hour, or until the crust is golden brown. (from *The Pioneers*)

Trail Breakfast

a. Explain to students that a trail breakfast might include pancakes, bacon, and coffee. Some days, breakfast included beans greased with slab bacon baked at a low temperature through the night.

b. Hold a trail breakfast. Have students help in the preparations. Invite parents or another class to the meal.

The Arts and the Overland Trail

Travel to the West over the Overland Trail was long and tedious. It took months for the emigrants to get to Oregon and California. To pass the time, the travelers would sing songs, dance, play music, write, and draw.

1. Music on the Trail

a. If possible, find recordings of songs played and sung on the trail, such as "Buffalo Gals," "Oh, Susanna!" and "Sweet Betsy from Pike." See the bibliography on pages 11–16 for books that have songs and music printed in them.

b. Invite the music teacher to help students learn songs the pioneers and forty-niners might have sung at night. Or, teach the songs to students yourself.

c. Provide a tape recorder and tape the songs as you and students sing them. Or, have students sing the songs at a performance for friends and family.

2. Photographs, Pictures, and Drawings

a. Encourage students to find pictures and photographs of life along the trail.

b. Invite students to sketch or draw anything the pioneers might have seen or done on the trail. Drawings might be based on pictures students have seen in books, software programs, or on the Internet.

c. Mount and display the artwork and photographs. Hold a class meeting to talk about what students learned from the pictures and photographs.

3. Reader's Theatre

a. Have students read a Reader's Theatre script and then talk about the various speaking styles of the characters. (See page 16 for information on obtaining Reader's Theatre scripts.)

b. Form small groups of students. Divide the script so each group has a section. Each student within each group can take a role in the Reader's Theatre story. Provide time for students to rehearse reading the roles. Encourage students to act out the roles to sound as they think the characters would sound.

c. Have groups present the script in sequence. Give them time afterward to compare the different interpretations. Invite students to present a performance for other classes.

Telling Stories and Writing

Stories, journal entries, and letters from home were important to the emigrants and pioneers as they traveled. They relied on travel guides written by others to make their way across North America. Their journal entries and letters home made a record of the times as well as helped them pass the time on their journeys. Invite your students to use their imagination and writing skills to write stories about what they think travel was like on the trail and to make their own Westward Travel Guide.

1. Letters to Relatives and Friends

a. Explain to students that the emigrants and pioneers were able to mail and receive letters from family and friends at the forts along the way, such as Forts Kearny, Laramie, and Boise.

b. Ask students to assume a role of someone on wagon train, or a steamer, or one of the Orphan Train children writing to someone at home.

Encourage students to write letters about what they are doing, what they are seeing, and any illnesses, as well as write about their feelings and thoughts, as that character. The letters should be written from the point of view of the role they have assumed.

c. Ask students to write the name of the persons to whom they have written on a card. Put all the cards in a box. Then have each student draw a card. Students should then receive the letter that was written to the person whose name is on the card.

2. You Were There

a. Invite students to tell the story about something that could have happened on the western trails, on a steamer, or on an Orphan Train.

To get ideas for their stories, ask them to review the notes in their journals; think about what they have read, heard, and viewed; and reflect on the class activities.

b. Meet with each student to ensure that the stories lend themselves to dramatic storytelling.

c. Encourage each student to rehearse his or her story with a partner.

d. Then divide the class into small groups with four or five storytellers in each group.

e. As each storyteller in each group shares his or her story, record the stories on tape. Place the tapes in the resource center so students can hear all of them.

3. A Westward Travel Guide to Oregon, Utah, and California

a. Talk with students about what they think travel guides to the West were like. Did they think they were accurate? What kinds of things were in the travel guides? Who wrote them?

b. As a group, write a Westward Travel Guide for the trip west. List topics students want to include in their travel guide. Write the list on a large sheet of paper and post it in the writing center. Topics might include:

- information about the types of wagons and extra supplies needed for the wagons.
- tools and ammunition needed.
- amount of food needed for each adult.
- a description of landmarks along the trail.
- distances between landmarks.
- a description of the rivers and where and how to cross them.
- tips on how to stay healthy on the trail.
- suggested remedies for illnesses.
- how to treat snakebites.
- medicines—what they do and what kind of medicines to take for certain ailments.

- plants that could help heal.
- suggestions for cooking along the trail.
- kinds of weather to expect on the prairie, in the desert, and in the mountains.
- how to take wagons up and down steep mountain areas.

c. Include a section in the Westward Travel Guide about the sea routes as well.

d. As a group, compare the topics with students' search questions. Were all topics researched? If additional topics need to be researched, invite students to get into their original migration groups to locate the information and record it.

e. Suggest that students individually or with a partner select a topic that relates to their search questions.

f. As students in each group are ready to draft their section, hold a class meeting to determine the format of the travel guide.

g. Ask students to reread their notes for their question and topic. After reading, ask students to write for ten minutes. Have them to share their writing with their partners and then with their small groups. Both partners and small groups should share the positive points of the writing regarding clarity and descriptiveness. They can also make suggestions for improvement.

Dear Matthew,
Today was a very difficult day
due to many steep hills. The Watsons
broke an axle and while Father helped
them, Rebecca and I collected dry bru
for tonights fire. The last few nights
have been very cold, so cold that even
our dog wants to sleep with us, though
Mother forbids it.
Father says that we may reach
Chimney Rock tomorrow! I will
write again soon. Your friend,
Charles Lake

The authors should consider the group suggestions. Encourage students to incorporate the suggestions into their writing. Again, the authors should write and rewrite for ten minutes, then share with a new partner and a new group. Authors can use any suggestions in their final draft.

h. After each group has drafted their sections, students are ready to put together their Westward Travel Guide. Encourage students to volunteer to serve on the following committees to publish the travel guide:

- **Editing Committee**—reads each section of the travel guide for clarity and accuracy.
- **Layout and Format Committee**—organizes and arranges how the pages and sections of the travel guide will look.
- **Publication Committee**—assists in assembling the travel guide by choosing which pages go where and actually putting the travel guide together.
- **Promotional Committee**—writes and publishes advertisements for the travel guide. They might promote the guide in other classrooms and with their families.

You may choose to have adult or student volunteers come to your class to help make the travel guide. Appoint one adult volunteer to oversee each committee in making the guide.

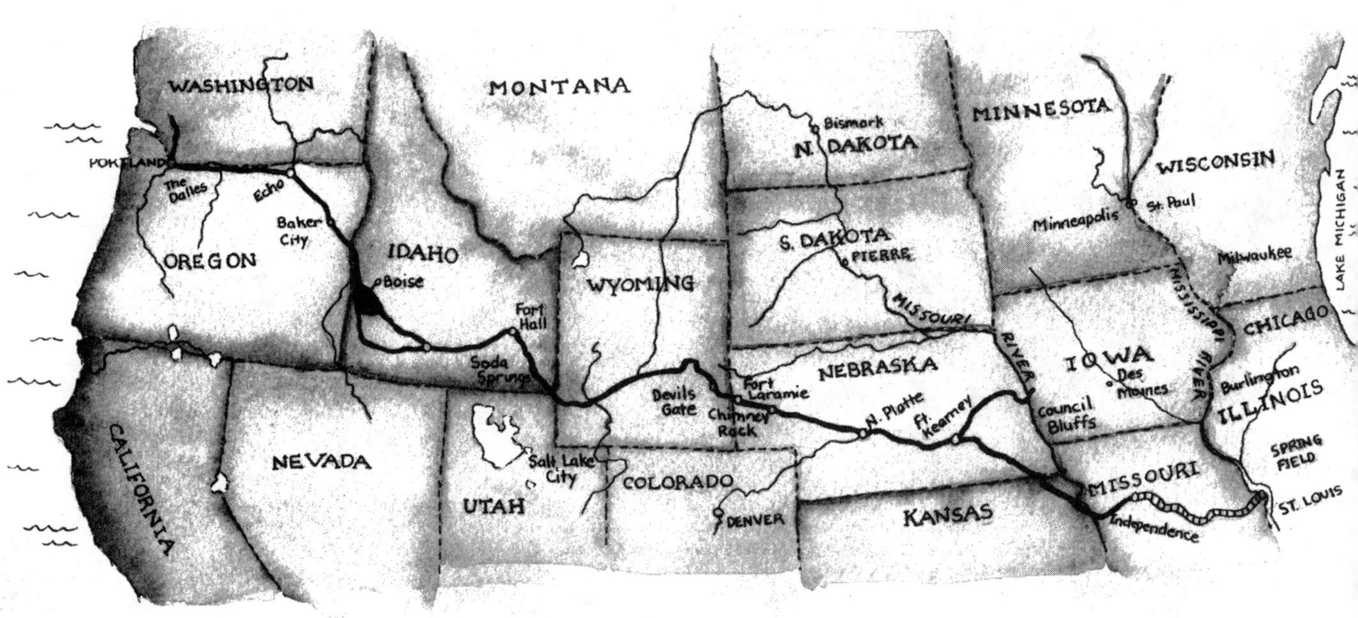

The United States: 1840-1870

What else was happening in the United States between 1840 and 1870? Who was president? Who were the people who did not migrate west? Give students the opportunity to research that time in the history of the United States.

Researching Thirty Years

a. Pique students' curiosity about what else was happening in the United States between 1840 and 1870 as the emigrants and pioneers were traveling west. Write each of the following in a special location on a bulletin board or chalkboard. Challenge students to find out the importance of each.

- Fifty-Four, Forty, or Fight
- Manifest Destiny
- Oregon Fever
- Orphan Train
- Forty-Niners
- Mormon Pioneers
- Abraham Lincoln
- First Transcontinental Railroad

b. Ask students to volunteer to learn more about one of the above topics. Form small collaborative teams of four or five students. Give each group a topic, and encourage students to learn when each of the events took place and several key points about each topic. Have students record key points through writing, drawings, or photographs.

c. Hold a class meeting so team can present its information to the class. Have students post the date and the information about their event on a time line.

d. Encourage students to locate dates of other events between 1840 and 1870, and why they think these events were important. Each date and event should be shared with the class and added to the time line.

Historical Time Line

Name________________

1869	First transcontinental train completed. The train did not stop travel over the Oregon Trail
1854	Kansas-Nebraska Act opened up these territories for settlement.
1850	Peak year of travelers—approximately 55,000 people went west.
1849–50	Gold rush in California.
1848	End of war with Mexico. This resulted in California and the Southwest becoming part of the United States. Gold found in the United States.
1846	Beginning of the war with Mexico. 49th parallel became the border between the United States and Canada. Oregon Territory now belonged to the United States. Expansionists used the slogan "fifty-four, forty, or fight."
1840–70	Between 250,000 and 500,000 people went west on the Oregon Trail.
1843	More than 1,000 settlers left Independence, Missouri, for Oregon.
1841	Small wagon trail led by John Bidwell left Independence, Missouri. At Soda Springs, Idaho, half of the people left the trail and went on to California on the Hedspeth Cutoff. The other half went to Oregon. It was the first overland wagon train to make the entire trip.
Late 1830s	Missionaries began developing what would become known as the Oregon Trail.
1812	Robert Stuart, a trapper, and six companions discovered the South Pass and the trails along the Sweetwater and Platte Rivers. It became a gateway for migration along the Oregon Trail.
1803	The United States bought the land between the Mississippi River and the Rocky Mountains from France—the "Louisiana Purchase."

Stories of People Who Went West

Emigrating to Oregon

Emily and William Dorn lived with their parents on a farm in Illinois. For the second year in a row, wind and lack of rain ruined much of the crops. Crops that could be sold would not bring enough money for the family to live on. Joseph Dorn, their father, was worried. They had already used up most of their credit at the store and the family's food might not carry them through the winter. Many a night, Emily and William saw their father deep in thought. Sometimes, after they went to bed, they heard their parents talk in soft, concerned voices. One cold, blustery day in January, 1844, Joseph received a letter from his brother in Oregon. His brother described the wonderful growing conditions for crops in the Oregon Territory. Land was available to anyone who wanted to work it. That night, Joseph and his wife, Eliza, sat pondering whether they should continue to try to make farming work in Illinois or whether they should join a wagon train to Oregon.

Early the next morning, Joseph set off for town. When Emily and William got home from school, their father still was not home. William and Emily started their chores—feeding the cows and horses. Finally, later that night, father came home. He had bought a prairie schooner! The family was going to Oregon, he said. Emily and William were excited.

Orphan Train Children

The Turner family lived in New York City. Mr. and Mrs. Turner had three children—Jeremiah, who was ten; his sister, Maria, age nine; and seven-year-old James. Mr. Turner didn't earn much money, but the family had enough to get by. Then Mr. Turner became very ill and could not work. Within a short time, he died. Now there was no money for the family. Mrs. Turner got a job working from sun up to sun down. Still, she didn't earn enough money to pay the rent and buy food. Jeremiah got a job in a restaurant so that the family had food. Maria took care of the house and looked after her little brother, James. One very sad day, a tragedy occurred. Mrs. Turner was coming home from her job when she was killed by a runaway horse and buggy. Now there was no one to take care of the children. What were they to do?

Mrs. Burk, a neighbor, had heard that trains took children to live with adoptive families in small towns and farms in the Midwest. Early one morning, Mrs. Burk took Jeremiah, Maria, and James to the train station. Within a few minutes, a train pulled into the station, and the conductor got out.

"Oh, you must be going west. My, you children look nice. Well, good luck." Mrs. Burk showed the children where to sit. Then she wished them well and waved good-bye. The train began to move very slowly. Gradually, it picked up speed. The children held each others' hands. Each of them were holding back tears trying to smile and to reassure each other. What would become of them? Would someone out west want them?

A Forty-Niner

It was 1849. Sam McQuire was reading the *New York Herald* newspaper when he saw an advertisement that made him stop and read the ad again and again. The ad said that gold—an inexhaustible supply of gold!—had been discovered in California. Gold could be picked up in lumps or scooped up in a pan. Could this be true?

In the same paper was an ad for the *David Crockett,* a steamer that sailed regularly to California. It was scheduled to sail in one week. Sam McQuire decided he had to go. He quit his job as a druggist. He decided against the 17,000-mile trip around Cape Horn of South America. Instead, he paid $350 to sail through the Isthmus of Panama.

Sam became an argonaut—a person who traveled to California by boat during the gold rush. The steamer was crowded. In fact, Sam shared a cabin with fifteen other people. Many people who took the Panamanian route got tropical diseases and became very sick. Some even died.

Upon arriving in Panama, Sam had to pay for transportation across the Isthmus. He then went upriver in a canoe. The last few miles he had to walk, watching for snakes and wild animals. Once he got to the Pacific side of the Isthmus, Sam found there were not enough boats to take everyone up the west coast to San Francisco. He had to wait ten days for a steamship.

Finally, Sam reached San Francisco with just two dollars in his pocket. He had expected to find rivers overflowing with gold. He was disappointed. Miners searched for gold at bends in a stream or used a pickax to break up rocks for a small vein of gold. This is not what the newspaper ad had said. Had he made a mistake?

Moving to Utah

Sarah and Joshua Livingston lived in Nauvoo, Illinois, with their family. Joshua was two when his family moved west with the rest of the Mormons. Sarah was born shortly after the family moved to Nauvoo. The Mormons, a religious group, wanted to live by themselves. They had settled along the Mississippi River in the southern part of Illinois in 1839.

The Mormons worked hard, building homes and schools. In the middle 1840s, the Mormons began to be persecuted. Joseph Smith, their leader, was killed by a mob of people. It was no longer safe to stay in Illinois. Their new leader, Brigham Young, decided that the Mormons had to move to Utah.

The families hurried to get ready to leave. They wanted to wait until April, but it was not safe to stay in Nauvoo. In February, 1846, about 15,000 Mormons crossed the Mississippi River into Iowa. The Livingstons traveled with a group of ten other families. They started across Iowa, but the weather was not good. The group decided to stop in Iowa. Soon more and more people joined them. They built homes and planted crops.

In 1847, the Mormons in Iowa heard that Brigham Young, with 73 Mormon wagons, had reached Utah Territory. They also learned that the first Mormons were putting up signposts to guide other Mormons to Utah. Joshua and Sarah knew that their family would soon leave Iowa and follow the trail west to Utah.

Vocabulary

argonauts - men and women who traveled to California by boat during the gold rush. Newspapers called California-based travelers "argonauts" after the gold-seeking heroes of ancient Greek mythology.

buffalo chips - dried buffalo dung used to make fires for cooking. They were sometimes used by children to throw like Frisbees.

emigrants - early pioneers to the West were emigrants because they left American soil and went to territories owned by Britain or Mexico.

forty-niners - those who took part in the 1849 California Gold Rush.

immigrant - one who comes into another country to become a resident.

jumping-off places - towns on the Missouri River from which the emigrants and pioneers started their trek west.

Manifest Destiny - John O'Sullivan, a New York newspaper man, wrote in 1845 that it was a mission ordained by God that the people in America should settle all of the land between the Atlantic and Pacific oceans throughout the North American continent. The Manifest Destiny ignored the Native Americans.

meeting the elephant - expression emigrants used to describe the very worst conditions possible.

nooning - time during the middle of the day when the wagon train stopped. Lunch was eaten, and the oxen were set loose to feed. The men checked the harnesses for breaks, and the cattle for sores. The women washed clothing. Wagons started again by 2:00 P.M.

Oregon fever - a longing and desire to go to Oregon.

"Oregon or Bust" - a slogan the emigrants shouted thinking about the new land.

overlanders - emigrants and pioneers who went west by land.

pioneer - one of the first people to settle a new territory.

prairie schooner - wagons that the emigrants and settlers took west.

slam johns - pancakes.

sowbelly - side pork or bacon.

Simulations

The simulation activities here will actively engage students in some of the same decisions the emigrants and pioneers made. To make their decisions, students will use the information from their search questions, the Westward Travel Guide, and the materials in the resource center as needed.

1. Divide the class into groups of five to seven students. Each group will be a family who is part of a wagon train. This allows each group to make its own decisions, just as the members of each wagon train in the 1800s made its own decisions.
2. Make a number of copies of the simulation cards (pages 57–75). Glue and laminate the cards to large index cards for durability.
3. To begin the simulation, give each group one family simulation card. This will give them some background information. Family members should decide who they are and their ages, and record this information in their logs.
4. Each family should then go through all the simulation cards in order from 1 through 13. Then, as each family decides what route they will take on card 14—Oregon or California—give each group the next appropriate card. Students should make their decisions as a family for each card. To make decisions, students can use information they collected for their research questions, the Westward Travel Guide they wrote, or additional information from resource materials.
5. After each decision is made, members of each family should jot down their decision and the reasons for the decision in their logs. Students should write in character—from the point of view of who they are within the family.
6. Several times a week, bring several wagon-train families together to talk about where they are on the trail, their experiences, what they have seen, and how they are feeling.

Simulation Cards

Give your students an opportunity to role-play family members emigrating to the West. Explain to students that boys and girls had special jobs they did in those days. Most often, the girls and their mothers cooked, cleaned, and took care of the house. The boys and their fathers hunted, gathered wood, and took care of the animals. Have a discussion with children about how things have changed now. Below and in the following pages, are a number of simulation cards to use with your students.

Family Card

Your family lives in Illinois. Wind and rain have damaged the crops for three years. There is little money and little food because of the crop failure. Your father has decided to move the family to Oregon. There must be a better life. In addition to your parents, there are four children in the family.

Decide who each of you is. Give yourselves names, decide your ages, and write them on the character page.

Family Card

Your family lives in Ohio. Your father is a blacksmith. There is plenty of work, but the crops are so poor, the farmers do not have any money to pay for work. Your father has just heard about all the gold in California. He decides the family must go. In your family there is a father, mother, and three children.

Decide who each of you is. Give yourselves names, decide your ages, and write them on the character page.

Family Card

Relatives have written your family about the land available in Oregon to anyone who wants to farm it. Crops are easy to grow. It is a plentiful land. Your father is tired of the difficulty of farming in Missouri and decides to try Oregon. There are seven members in your family—a father, mother, four children, and a hired man.

Decide who each of you is. Give yourselves names, decide your ages, and write them on the character page.

Family Card

Your father is restless. You are always moving, from Pennsylvania to Indiana, then to Missouri. Your father has been hearing about gold in California. You are going west. Your family includes a father, mother, three boys, and two girls.

Decide who each of you is. Give yourselves names, decide your ages, and write them on the character page.

Card 1

Fathers:

- Decide what you will do with your land.
- What type of wagon are you going to get? How large is your wagon? Where will you get it?
- What spare parts will you take for the wagon?
- Are you going to use oxen or mules to pull the wagon?
- What tools are you going to take?
- What animals are you going to take?
- How much money do you think the family will need to get to Oregon?
- Decide how your sons will help you get ready for the trip. Work together in getting ready.
- How long will it take for your family to get ready to go?

Card 1

Mothers:

- The family is moving to Oregon. Make your packing list.
- What foods are you going to take along?
- How much of everything are you going to take?
- What cooking utensils will you take?
- What clothes and how much clothing will you take for each member of the family?
- What kind of bedding will you need?
- What medicines will you take along?
- Will you take any furniture? If so, what will you take? What will you have to leave behind?
- Decide how your daughters can help you get ready for the trip. Work together in getting ready. What are you going to do?

Card 2

Fathers:
Your jumping-off place to Oregon is Independence, Missouri. Your task is to join a wagon train. Meet with the other men trying to join one of the wagon trains. Who are these men? Where did they come from? Each of the fathers are wagon captains who make the decisions about the wagon trains. As wagon captains, what are your responsibilities? Decide when the wagon train will start for Oregon. What weather conditions are you looking for? With your family, decide on a name for your wagon train.

Card 2

Children:
You are in Independence, Missouri. You have met some of the other children who are waiting to join one of the wagon trains. Who are they? How old are they? Where did they come from? What can you find out about them? How do they feel about going west?

Card 2

Mothers:
You are in Independence, Missouri. You have met with the other mothers who are waiting to join one of the wagon trains. Compare what you have packed for the trip. Talk about where you have come from. What are some of your concerns about the trip? What do you want to know about the other families on the wagon train?

Card 2

Families:

You are ready to leave Independence. Mark Independence, Missouri, on your map. On what date, month, and year did you leave Independence?

Your family will work together in marking the trail from Independence to Oregon. While you will be working together, each member of your family should have his or her own map.

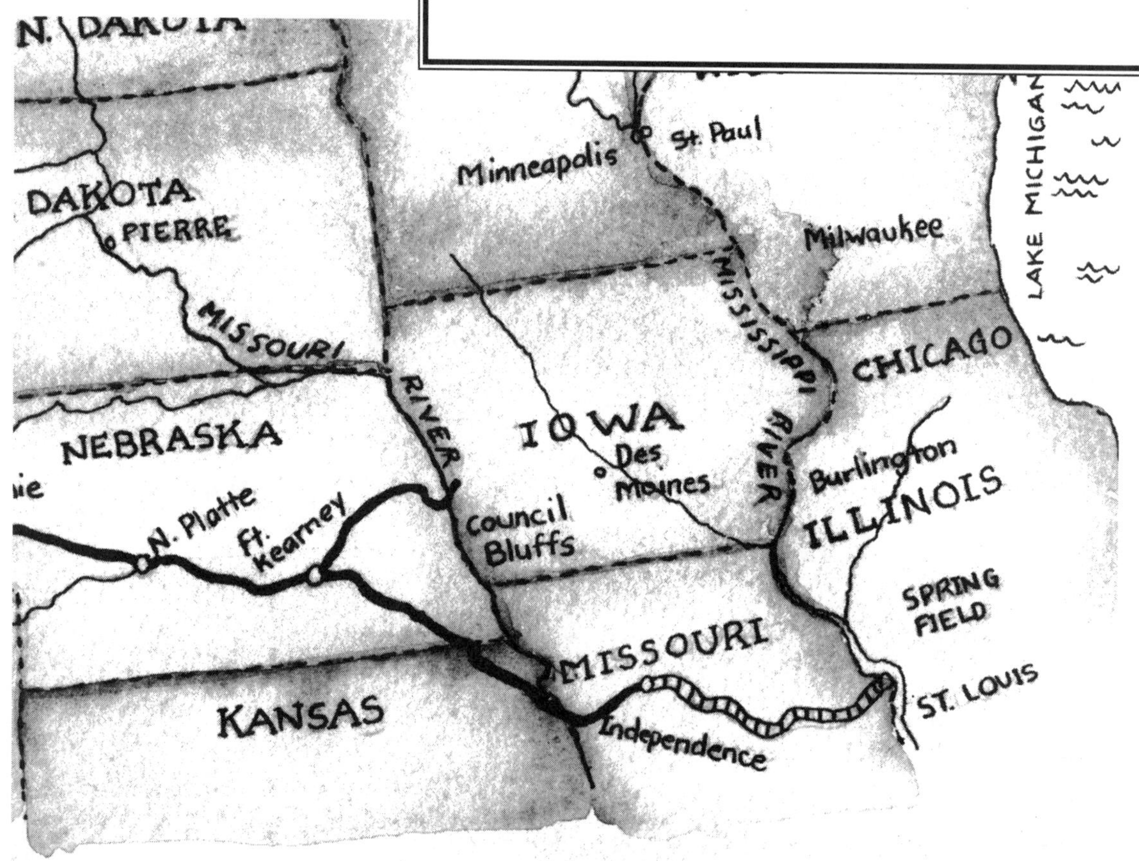

Card 3

Families:
The wagon train has been on the trail for three weeks. About how many miles does your wagon travel each day? How far has the wagon train gone? The wagon train went through Alcove Springs to Fort Kearny and along the south bank of the Platte River. How far is Fort Kearny from Independence, Missouri?

How do each of you feel? How do your feet feel?

Card 4

Fathers / Wagon Captains:
What is the daily routine on the trail? What time does the day start? What time does the wagon train begin to roll out of camp? When does the wagon train stop so that people can eat? What time does the wagon train stop at night?

Card 5

Mothers and Daughters:

The wagon train has stopped for the night. What are you going to cook for the evening meal? Are you going to have any hot foods? If yes, what do you need to start a fire? Does each family cook for itself or does everyone on a wagon train eat together?

Card 5

Sons:

Boys' jobs are to keep the cattle fed and watered, milk the cows, and hunt and fish. What do you feed the cattle? Where do you get it? How do you find water for them? What do you do with the milk? What do you do with the wagons in the morning?

Card 5 

Fathers / Wagon Captains:
How many wagons need repair? What is wrong with them? Do the people have the parts for the repair? How are you getting the men to help each other? What have you heard about the trail ahead?

Card 5 

Families:
Describe what the people do in the wagon train before they go to bed. Describe the morning activities from the time everyone wakes up until the wagon train is on the trail.

Card 6

Families:
You are now about 480 miles west of the Missouri River, and you have been on the trail about one month. You are following the Platte River. What kind of terrain do you see? Are there any flowers, or trees? What kind of grass is available for the cattle?

Card 7

Fathers / Wagon Captains:
The wagon train is ready to cross one of the rivers. There are four wagon trains with 100 wagons waiting to cross before your wagon train can cross, and there is no ferry. Talk with the other wagon masters.

- How are the wagons going to get across?
- How will you get all the things in the wagons across?
- How are the women and children going to get across?
- Who will take the cattle across?

Card 8

Families:
There are many landmarks along the route through the Nebraska Territory to Fort Laramie. Choose one of the following landmarks at which your wagon train will stop for a day. Mark it on your map. Why did you choose this landmark? What is it like? How are you spending your time?

- Courthouse Rock
- Chimney Rock
- Scotts Bluff

Card 9

Families:
You have reached Fort Laramie. This is one of the few stops along the trail where you can buy supplies, mail and receive letters, receive expert help in fixing your wagons, and get information about the best river crossings ahead, as well as information about weather conditions, local Native Americans, and cholera outbreaks.

- What do you want to do at this fort?
- What needs to be repaired?
- Are you buying supplies? How do the prices compare with the prices where you came from at Fort Kearny?
- What have you learned about the conditions on the trail?
- Did you mail any letters? To whom? Did you receive any mail? From whom?

Card 10

Families:

People on your wagon train have experienced and are continuing to experience problems. Choose two problems from the groups listed below that people on your wagon train are experiencing, and describe what is happening.

- Sickness—cholera, dysentery, mumps, measles, death.
- Danger—snakebites, drowning, shootings, children falling out of or under wagons.
- Bad weather—terrible wind and lightning storms. Many of the cattle are scattered. Mud is up to the hub of the wheels.
- Water problems—shortage of water or polluted water.

Card 11

Families:

You have your first encounter with Native Americans. Everyone is eager to see the Native Americans, but people on the wagon train are also a little afraid. The Native Americans are in small groups. Women are with the men. They want to trade berries, beads, moccasins, meat, and bullets. Will you trade with the Native Americans. If so, what will you trade?

Card 12

Families:
You have come to Independence Rock. What do you know about this rock? What did you write on the rock? How did you do it?

Card 13

Families:
Your wagon train has now reached South Pass and the Continental Divide. Why is the Continental Divide so important? What are your feelings about where you are in your travels?

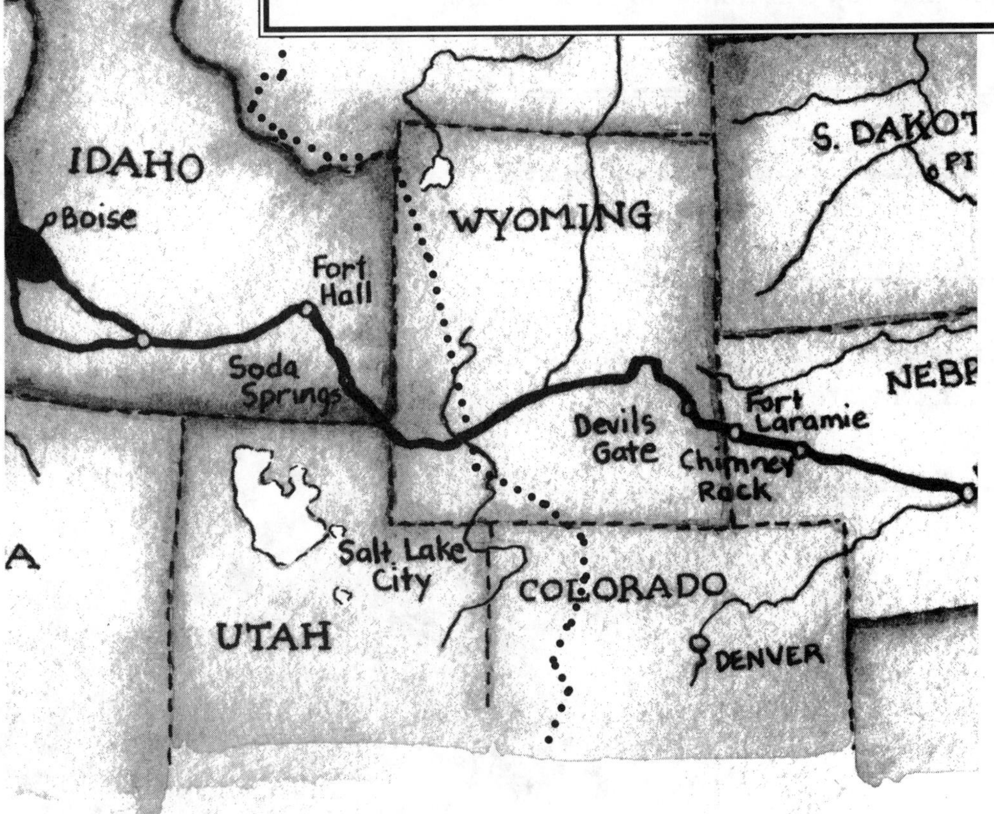

Card 14 

Families:
You now have to decide which way you are going along the westward trail. You can either go farther northwest into Oregon, or you can split off and go southwest toward California. Which will it be?

Oregon Card 15 

Families:
Decide whether you need supplies and must stop at Fort Bridger or whether you can take Sublette's Cutoff.

California Card 15 

Families:
You may stop at Fort Bridger and then go on to Salt Lake City. If you stop at Fort Bridger, why are you stopping?

California Card 16

Families:
The wagon train is traveling along the Humboldt River, which is about 290 miles long. The grass supply is so short that you are afraid the livestock will not have enough to eat. Alkaline dust is irritating everyone's throats and eyes. How are you feeding your livestock?

Oregon Card 16

Fathers / Wagon Captains:
You are continuing northwest. Decide whether you are going to stop at one of the following places. If you stop, why are you stopping?

- Soda Springs
- Fort Hall
- Fort Boise

Oregon Card 17

Mothers:

The wagon master has just informed you how the wagon train will cross the Snake River. What do you need to do to protect the children, the clothing, the food, and all the goods you have brought with you? What can the children do to help? Talk with them about what they need to do.

Oregon Card 17

Fathers / Wagon Captains:

The Snake River is just ahead. You will travel about 250 miles along the south side of the river. The Snake River is very difficult to cross. The common crossing is shallow, but about 600 feet wide and moves very swiftly. There is one small ferry that takes wagons across. Sometimes it takes days to get across. Native Americans swim the river from morning to night and can assist for a price. You can also chain the wagons together to cross or take the wagons apart and float them across the river. What is your decision? How will you get the women and children across? How will you get the cattle across? Inform your families of your decision.

California Card 17

Families:
You are at the Humboldt Sink. The only water supply is from springs and geysers that spout boiling hot, stinking water. You are hot and exhausted. Just beyond this is the Forty Mile Desert where nothing grows and there is no water. What do you have to do to be able to go across the desert? How will you feed the cattle?

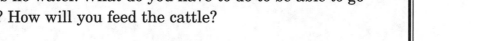

Oregon Card 18

Families:
The wagon train has passed Fort Boise and is now approaching the Blue Mountains. The oxen are tired and are having a hard time pulling the wagon. The oxen will never be able to pull the wagon over the mountains. You are going to have to leave some things along the trail. What are you going to leave? This must be a family decision.

Write a "roadside telegraph"—a message that you will leave for wagons that are following you. Write your message on sun-bleached bones or paper, and post it on a stick.

California Card 18

Fathers / Wagon Captains:
You must travel across the desert in one stretch. When are you going to travel—night or day?

Families:
The hot earth is burning your feet. You are very hungry, thirst-crazed, and frightened for your lives as you cross this desert. What keeps you going? Why don't you just stop and lie down next to your oxen?

Card 19

Families:
Your family has just been told that the train is ready to cross the mountains. The trail is rocky in places. In other places, the ruts are very deep. Some wagon wheels have gotten stuck in the ruts. Part of the mountain trail is very steep. You have heard that in some wagon trains, the wagon wheels have been taken off and the wagons let down with ropes. After considering all the options, what are you going to do?

Oregon Card 20

Families:
You have finally arrived in Oregon. You are thankful you made it. It is now the middle of October and the start of the rainy season. Your family has very little money. Food is scarce, and you have very few clothes. As a family, decide what you must do to survive the first winter in Oregon.

California Card 20 

Fathers:
You have arrived in Sacramento and you're ready to dig for gold. Where are you going? Are you going to a mine or a stream? What tools do you need?

California Card 20 

Mothers:
You have heard that you should start a business for yourself. What will you do—cook, bake, clean, iron, sew, or start a boarding house? What other ideas do you have? Decide what you will do and how much you will charge. How are your daughters going to help you?

Name ____________________________________

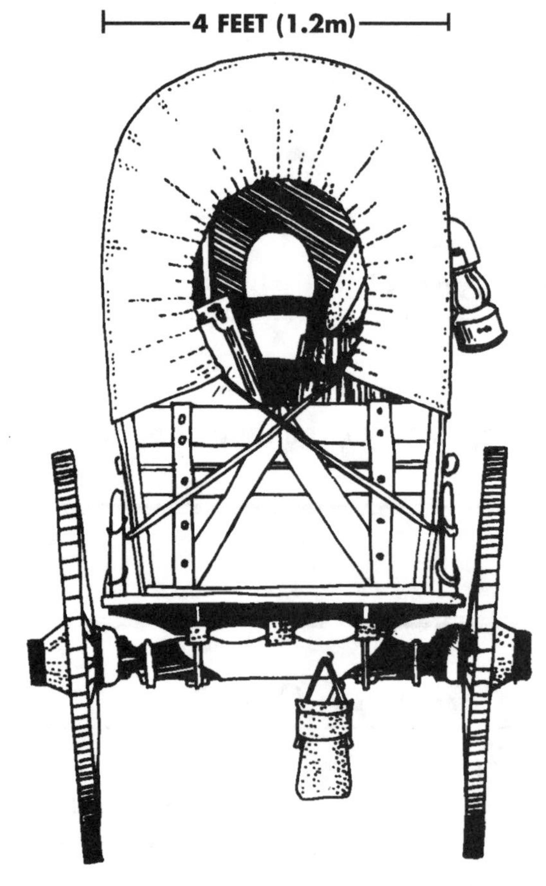

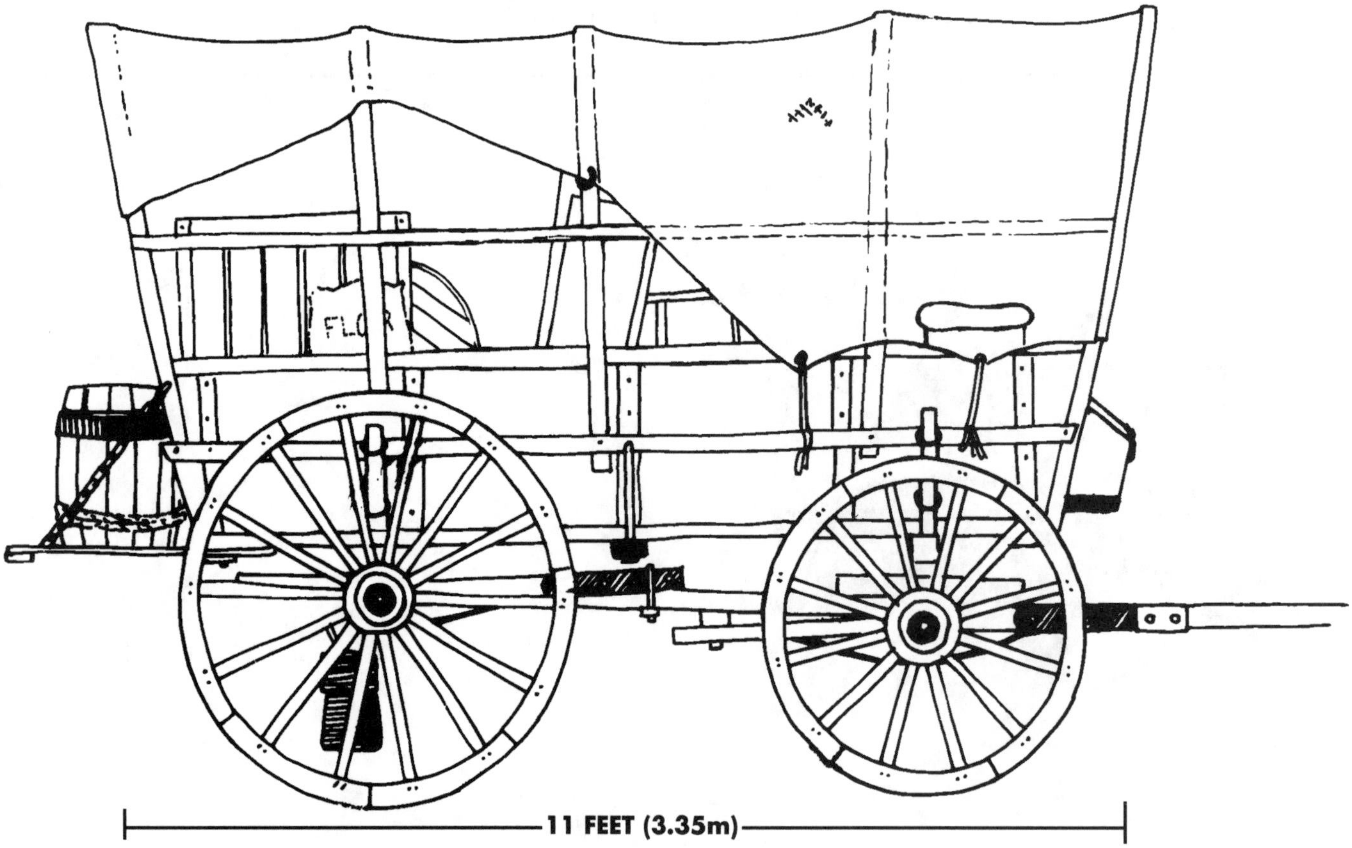

11 FEET (3.35m)

Oregon and California Trail Map

Name ______________________________

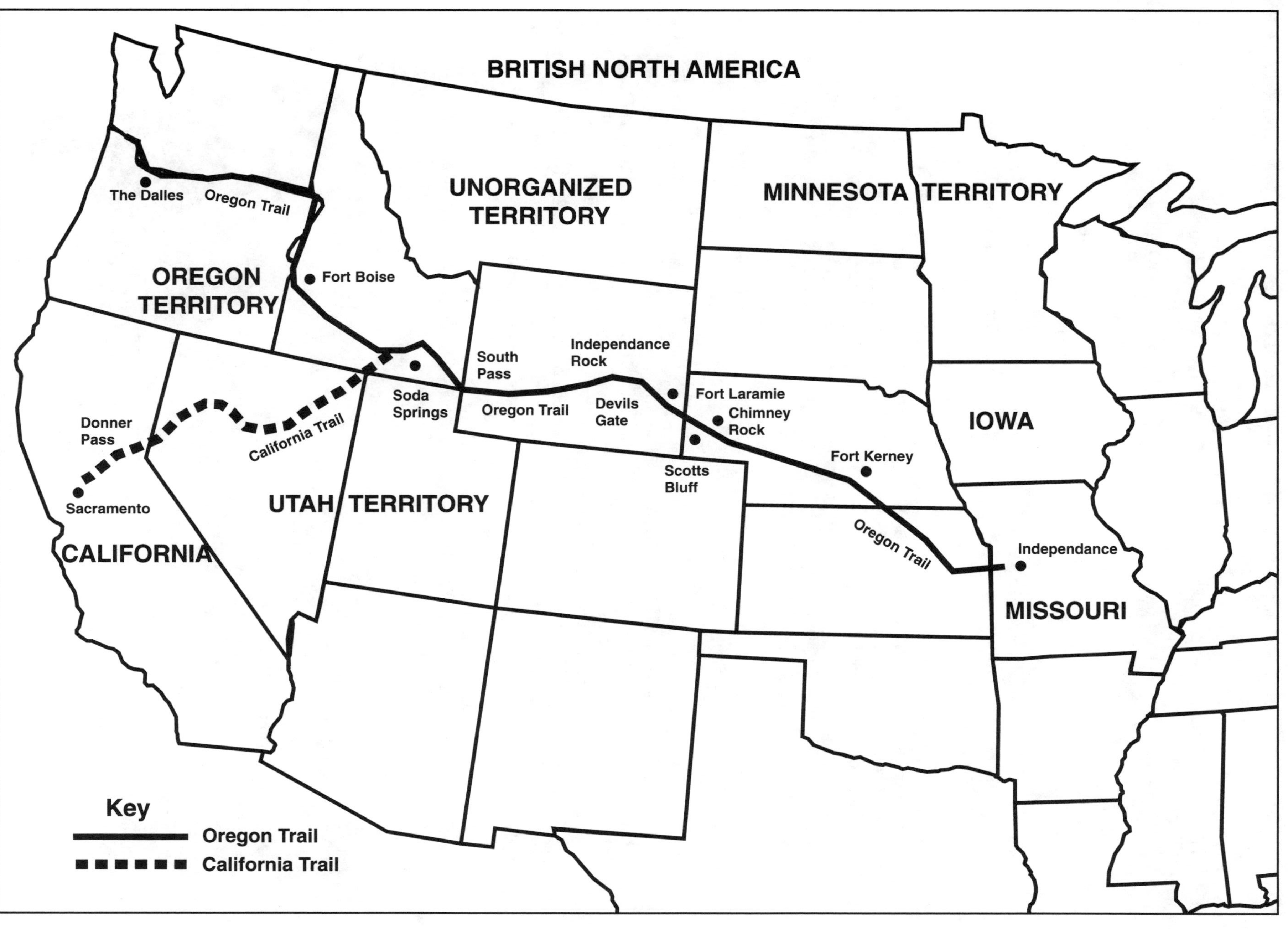

Photo References

Cover — Solomon D. Butcher Collection, Nebraska Historical Society, B983-2938 (Emigrants entering the Loup Valley in Custer County, Nebraska, 1886)

Title Page — Solomon D. Butcher Collection, Nebraska Historical Society, B983-2938

pg. 19 — Solomon D. Butcher Collection, Nebraska Historical Society, B983-2938C (Emigrants moving into Custer County, Nebraska, 1886)

pg. 21 — Solomon D. Butcher Collection, Nebraska Historical Society, B983-2938A (Emigrants at Gates Post Office,Custer County, Nebraska, 1886)

pg. 24 — Solomon D. Butcher Collection, Nebraska Historical Society, B983-2938

pg. 27 — Solomon D. Butcher Collection, Nebraska Historical Society, B983-2938A

pg. 37 — Solomon D. Butcher Collection, Nebraska Historical Society, B983-2360A (Harvey Andrews family at grave of their child, Willie Andrews, age 19 months in Cedar Canyon, Nebraska. The cedars in Cedar Canyon made Mr. Andrews a rich man by selling cedar posts and ridge logs for the settlers' sod houses.)

pg. 46 — Solomon D. Butcher Collection, Nebraska Historical Society, B983-1669 (Southwest Custer County, Nebraska, near Arnold, 1892)

pg. 47 — Solomon D. Butcher Collection, Nebraska Historical Society, B983-2938A

pg. 52 — Solomon D. Butcher Collection, Nebraska Historical Society, B983-2214 (Sod school house, East Custer School, Custer County, Nebraska, 1888 or 1889)

pg. 54 — Des Moines River, Iowa. Red Lane Studio

pg. 54 — Solomon D. Butcher Collection, Nebraska Historical Society, B983-1250 (East Custer County, Nebraska, 1887 or 1888)

pg. 60 — Solomon D. Butcher Collection, Nebraska Historical Society, B983-2938

pg. 63 — Solomon D. Butcher Collection, Nebraska Historical Society, B983-2938C

pg. 64 — Solomon D. Butcher Collection, Nebraska Historical Society, B983-2938A

pg. 65 — Solomon D. Butcher Collection, Nebraska Historical Society, B983-2938C

pg. 68 — Solomon D. Butcher Collection, Nebraska Historical Society, B983-5159 (Native American camp at Pine Ridge, Nebraska. Photographed during the late Indian War, January 1891)

pg. 70 — Solomon D. Butcher Collection, Nebraska Historical Society, B983-1097 (McCaslin, Rose Valley, Nebraska, known as the "Preacher's" home.)

pg. 71 — Solomon D. Butcher Collection, Nebraska Historical Society, B983-1669

pg. 74 — Bridger Mountain Range. Red Lane Studio

Illustrations on pages 3, 4, 6, 11 and 16 reprinted from the following copyright-free text: Old Engravings and Illustrations, Volume I, People. Dick Sutphen. 1965.

Illustrations on page 38 reprinted from the following copyright-free text: Handbook of Early Advertising Art, Pictorial Volume, Third Edition, Dover Publications, 1956

Notes